Let's Get to Know
the Incas

by Jennifer Coates-Conroy

Editorial Offices: Glenview, Illinois • Parsippany, New Jersey • New York, New York
Sales Offices: Needham, Massachusetts • Duluth, Georgia • Glenview, Illinois
Coppell, Texas • Ontario, California • Mesa, Arizona

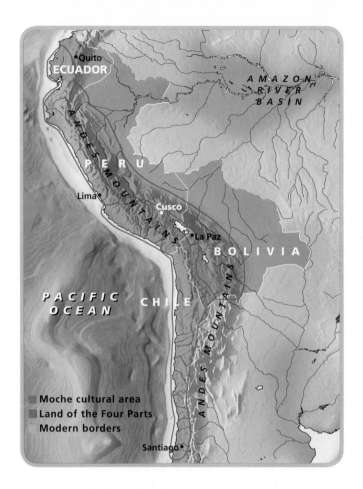

Moche cultural area
Land of the Four Parts
Modern borders

Where Did the Incas Begin?

Thousands of years ago, many different Indian peoples lived in the Andes Mountains in Peru. About A.D. 1200, the Quechuan Indians conquered these mountains and began to rule over the other peoples who lived there.

The Quechuan Indians migrated to the Andean area of South America. This area was an ideal place to live. It was far away from the jungle **thickets** and larger forests. It was also high up in the mountains, where the air was clean and pure. Living as one tribe, these people were called Incas, which means "Children of the Sun."

3

A Huge Empire

The Andean area, or the Inca empire, was huge! It extended through Peru, Ecuador, northwest Argentina, and a large part of Chile. The Incas made their capital city Cusco, which is right in the Peruvian highlands. Whenever a new emperor came to power, this is where he built his palace.

The capital city was full of all sorts and sizes of buildings. There were huge halls for entertainment. But the finest temples and palaces were smaller. Actually, most of the Inca buildings were only one story high. The **glorious** structures of the Incas were built for function, rather than for show. *Big* didn't mean "better." The Inca didn't build large buildings to show off their power or wealth. In fact, even the Inca emperor lived in a small palace.

The government was located in the central part of the Inca city. Regular citizens lived in the surrounding areas. Their homes were humble, rectangular-shaped buildings. The walls were made from hand-cut limestone or **granite** blocks. The roofs were made from thatched grass.

The First Inca Emperor

According to legend, the very first Inca emperor was Manco Capac. He lived around A.D. 1200.

Every Inca emperor after Manco Capac worshipped the sun and was considered to be a powerful god. Inca rulers, in fact, were thought to be the sun's representatives on Earth. For centuries, whenever the Incas conquered others, they insisted that those people worship the sun too.

Early Inca emperors

The Incas make offerings to the Sun.

Worshipping the Sun

The Incas believed that the sun was the reason for life. This made sun worship a part of the Inca culture. Many other people who lived in the Andes Mountains were also sun worshippers. *Inti,* the Sun, the father of the Incas, was the most important god in the Inca religion. The temples contained statues and images of Inti as well as many other gods and goddesses that the Incas worshipped.

Mama Quilla, also known as Mother Moon, was the Sun's wife and the mother of the Incas. Just as the Sapa Inca, or emperor, represented the sun on Earth, the Coya, or empress, represented the moon.

The last Inca emperor, Atahualpa, receives a Spanish missionary.

The Royal Inca Family

The royal family worshipped in the beautiful temples, but the people took part in open-air ceremonies in the city center. There, they offered treasures to the gods, such as leaves, feathers, and shells.

The emperor of the Incas was also the head of the imperial court at Cusco. If the emperor had a son, the boy became next in line to rule the throne. This boy was considered a living god. No ordinary person was good enough to teach him. That had to be done by his royal parents.

Inca society had strict levels of power. First, there was the Sapa. The Sapa's family members, including women, were advisors. Next came the temple priest, the architects, and the army commanders. At the lowest level, with the least power, were the craft workers, army captains, farmers, and herders.

Studying the Inca Calendar

Inca priests studied the sky and the seasons to create a calendar for the farmers. Although farmers were of the lowest class in Inca society, they were important because they supplied the Incas with food. Farmers worked long hours in the Peruvian farmlands. They dug canals to bring water to their crops on steep, **terraced** hillsides. This form of irrigation allowed water from the **torrents** created by rains and melting snow to reach the crops that needed it the most.

Maize, or corn, and potatoes were the main crops planted. The men dug holes in the ground, and the women dropped in seeds. As the maize shoots grew, boys used slingshots to frighten birds and animals away from the growing crops.

Levels of Inca society

The High Cost of Worship

If you were an Inca, you showed your respect to the emperor by paying tribute. This meant that you could donate food and goods to him. Inspectors visited the countryside to decide how much food and goods each area should send to the Inca emperor.

Another way of paying tribute was by working. If you were a male 25 years or older, you would have had to pay taxes, or tribute, with some form of labor. Often your whole family would work together to pay the tribute owed. Only the emperor's nobles, women, and officers were not required to work in the fields.

Sometimes rulers gave to the people instead of just taking from them. For example, architects, engineers, and craft workers received food, clothing, and materials as wages so that they could work full time for Inca rulers.

Gold, copper, silver, and tin were mined by the laborers.

The Conquistadors Conquer

The Spanish explorer Francisco Pizarro had heard stories of Inca gold. He came to South America with other Spaniards in hopes of finding these riches. These *conquistadors* landed in the late 1520s.

By using powerful weapons, the Spanish easily defeated the Incas, ending the centuries-old empire. Atahualpa was the last ruling Inca emperor.

Francisco Pizarro needed an army of only 168 men and some Indians to defeat the mighty Atahualpa. To avoid being ambushed, Pizarro took a dangerous route through the mountains. But when the Incas saw the Spaniards, they foolishly welcomed them. Atahualpa did not know of Francisco Pizarro's desire to rule the Inca empire.

Francisco Pizarro leads his conquistadors through the Andes mountains.

These gold-and-turquoise medals from a tomb in Peru date back to pre-Inca times.

The Incas Fight Back

When the Spanish conquered the Incas, they destroyed their cities, their religion, and their way of life. The Spanish also made the Incas their slaves.

But the Incas fought back for centuries. They hid the treasures they had intended for their gods deep in the Andes mountains, in an area that is now referred to as Machu Picchu.

These Peruvians are in native clothing.

Inca Traditions Remain

Today, **curiosity** about the Incas and their way of life bring many tourists to visit the Andes. Even now, in the remote mountains, some Inca traditions have survived. In the mountain villages of Peru and Bolivia, older people speak Quechua, the Inca language. The older villages and their people have also kept the traditions of Inca food, music, and religious customs.

Although the Inca empire ended almost 500 years ago, you can still see many Inca ideas in practice. For example, farmers still use the Inca irrigation techniques and farming methods.

A Visit to a Lost City

Modern trains take visitors to the **ruins** of Machu Picchu, the lost city of the Incas.

Do you want to see firsthand what an Inca might have looked like? Then visit the highlands of Peru. There are nearly 20 million Inca descendants living there. They still wear the same style of clothing as their ancestors, and they still follow the same way of life.

A tourist train winds through the mountains on its way to Machu Picchu.

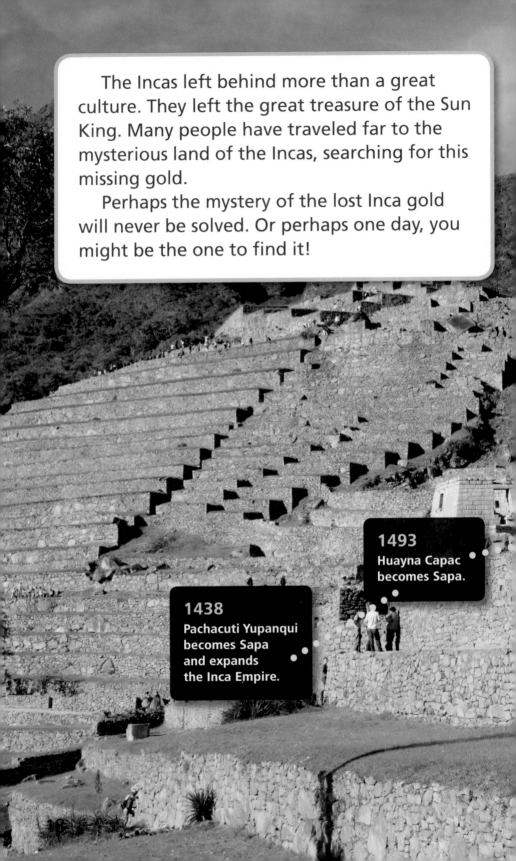

The Incas left behind more than a great culture. They left the great treasure of the Sun King. Many people have traveled far to the mysterious land of the Incas, searching for this missing gold.

Perhaps the mystery of the lost Inca gold will never be solved. Or perhaps one day, you might be the one to find it!

1493
Huayna Capac becomes Sapa.

1438
Pachacuti Yupanqui becomes Sapa and expands the Inca Empire.

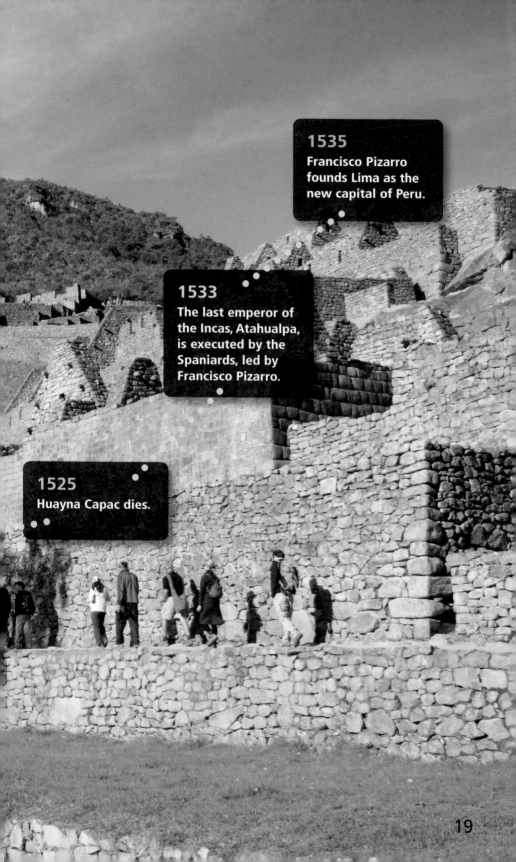

1535
Francisco Pizarro founds Lima as the new capital of Peru.

1533
The last emperor of the Incas, Atahualpa, is executed by the Spaniards, led by Francisco Pizarro.

1525
Huayna Capac dies.

Glossary

curiosity *n.* desire to know.

glorious *adj.* marked by great beauty or splendor.

granite *n.* very hard natural rock.

ruins *n.* destroyed or fallen down buildings.

terraced *adj.* formed into different levels.

thickets *n.* dense growths of small trees.

torrent *n.* a violent rushing stream.